MW01106538

How are they Made?
Plates and Mugs

Wendy Blaxland

MACMILLAN
LIBRARY

First published in 2008 by
MACMILLAN EDUCATION AUSTRALIA PTY LTD
15ñ19 Claremont Street, South Yarra 3141

Visit our website at www.macmillan.com.au or go directly to www.macmillanlibrary.com.au

Associated companies and representatives throughout the world.

National Library of Australia
Cataloguing-in-Publication data

Blaxland, Wendy, 1949-
    Plates and mugs / author, Wendy Blaxland.
    South Yarra, Vic. : Macmillan Education, 2008.
    ISBN: 978 1 4202 6414 2 (hbk.)
    Blaxland, Wendy, 1949- How are they made?
    Includes index.
    For primary age.
    Plates (Tableware)--Juvenile literature.
    Mugs--Juvenile literature.
    Tableware--Juvenile literature.
    Drinking vessels--Juvenile literature.
642.7

Edited by Anna Fern
Cover design, text design and page layout by Cristina Neri, Canary Graphic Design
Photo research by Legend Images
Map by Damien Demaj, DEMAP; modified by Cristina Neri, Canary Graphic Design

Printed in China

Acknowledgements

The author would like to thank the following people for their expert advice: Tony Conway, Head of Ceramics
Programme, La Trobe University, Australia; and Janet de Boos, Head of Ceramics, Australian National University.

The author and the publisher are grateful to the following for permission to reproduce copyright material:

Front cover photograph: Plate with yellow border, blue flowers © DNY59/iStockphoto; red mug © Jitalia17/iStockphoto;
4 coloured cups, stacked © Cat London/iStockphoto; plain white plate © bluestocking/iStockphoto. Images repeated
throughout title.

Photos courtesy of:
AAP Image/XINHUA, **7**; © Visual Arts Library (London)/Alamy, **6**; Janet DeBoos, The Australian National University, **16**
(bottom), **19** (top), **20**, **21** (top), **22** (bottom), **26** (bottom); Dinnerware Depot, Inc., www.dinnerwaredepot.com, **24**
(bottom), **25** (bottom); © Darklord_71/Dreamstime.com, **11** (bottom); © fux/fotolia, **23** (bottom); Getty Images/Digital
Vision/Ryan McVay, **29** (top); Getty Images/Brooke Slezak, **30** (bottom); © Jaroslaw Baczewski/iStockphoto, **5** (top);
© DNY59/iStockphoto, **3** (centre above and bottom), **10** (top left), **12** (top left, centre left and bottom left), **15** (bottom
right), **16** (bottom right), **19** (bottom), **22** (top), **23** (top), **24** (top), **25** (top), **27** (bottom), **29** (bottom), **30** (centre left),
31 (top), **32** (bottom); © Dieter K. Henke/iStockphoto, **4** (bottom right); © Blaz Kure/iStockphoto, **28** (right); © Andrew
Manley/iStockphoto, **5** (bottom); © ron sumners/iStockphoto, **4** (bottom left); © Irochka Tischenko/iStockphoto, **14**;
MuddyMountainPottery.com, **11** (top); Bill Lyons/Saudi Aramco World/PADIA, **27** (top); © ImageDJ/Alamy/Photolibrary, **8**
(right); JTB Photo/Photolibrary, **10** (bottom); © Jacky Naegelen/REUTERS/PICTURE MEDIA, **17**, **18**; Bill Reddick (shows the
making of Canada's State Dinnerware), **9** (bottom); Wikimedia Commons, photo by Petri Krohn, **8** (left).

Headshot illustrations accompanying textboxes throughout title © Russell Tate/iStockphoto.

Contents

Glossary words

When a word is printed in **bold**, you can look up its meaning in the Glossary on page 31.

From raw materials to products

Everything we use is made from raw materials from the Earth. These are called natural resources. People take natural resources and make them into useful products.

Mugs and plates

Mugs are sturdy, often decorated cups with handles. We drink from mugs. Plates of different sizes are used to serve food and eat from.

The main raw material used to make mugs and plates is clay, dug from the ground. The moist clay is shaped and then heated to high temperatures to dry and harden. Products made in this way are called **ceramics**.

Mugs and plates are usually covered by a hard, glossy coating called a **glaze**. The raw materials for glazes may be dug from the ground, or they may be made from chemicals.

This German beer mug has a lid to keep out flies.

Handmade mugs are as individual as their makers.

Plates can be individually decorated with many patterns and glaze finishes.

Why do we need mugs and plates?

Mugs are used for drinks, especially hot liquids. Plates of different sizes are used to serve food and to eat from. More liquid foods are served in bowls.

Ceramic mugs and plates are useful for holding liquids. The glazed surface of ceramic mugs and plates makes them **waterproof.**

Mugs and plates are made from many different types of clays and with different finishes. They may also be made of other materials, such as metal, wood, hard plastic, and even disposable paper with a waterproof coating. Not all cultures serve food on plates. Some use disposable 'plates' made of leaves or wrap food in bread.

A Japanese meal is often served on plates of different shapes and sizes.

The history of mugs and plates

For thousands of years, people in many different cultures have shaped clay into objects and used fire to harden them into pottery. In these cultures, ceramic containers are used as essential everyday items for storage, cooking and to eat from.

Question & Answer

Where did the term 'pothole' come from?

In Staffordshire, England, roads were sometimes built over deposits of fine clay. Potters dug 'potholes' in the roads and took the clay to make into pottery. If caught, they were fined.

Mugs and plates through the ages

10 000 BCE
Pottery develops separately in Japan, China and North Africa, then Russia, Mesopotamia (now Iraq), India and South America.

5000–6000 BCE
The first useful pottery is made in central Europe. Egyptians use pottery.

2400–2200 BCE
'Beaker pots', which are like mugs, are first used in Britain.

27 000–23 000 BCE
Small nude female figures are made of ceramics in the area now known as the Czech Republic.

30 000 BCE   10 000 BCE   8000 BCE   6000 BCE   0 CE   1000

10 500 BCE
The earliest known pottery containers are made in Japan.

4000–2000 BCE
The potter's wheel develops in Mesopotamia, speeding up the pottery process.

This pottery cup, made in ancient Greece in about 550 BCE, is decorated with an image of the god Zeus and an eagle.

This piece of pottery, recently dug up in China, gives us some clues about how people lived when it was made, about 700 years ago.

Guess What!

Pottery can help us study ancient cultures because it lasts much longer than other materials. How it is made and decorated can reveal information about everyday life, art and attitudes, especially in cultures without written records.

Early 1700s German potters develop porcelain.

Mid 1700s Pottery factories develop in England.

1300s Chinese porcelain is **imported** to England. German law insists mugs include a lid to keep out flies.

Late 1700s English potters use **moulds** to make pots all the same.

1897 Bone china is first developed by Josiah Spode, in England.

1500 CE
1600 CE
1700 CE
1800 CE
1900 CE
2000 CE

600s and 700s CE White **porcelain** is made in China.

1753 The English develop a mechanical way of putting patterns on china, called transfer ware.

1945 Factories begin using tunnel kilns. Pots are loaded on cars that travel through different sections of the **kiln** to be **fired** and cooled. This means pottery can be produced by less skilled operators. Pottery is also decorated by machines instead of skilled artists.

What are mugs and plates made from?

Mugs and plates are usually made of different clays coated with glazes. These glazes give them a glassy, waterproof surface. Mugs and plates are often decorated with patterns or words by hand or machine.

rim

border

booge

base

lip or rim

handle

body

base

This stoneware plate from Staffordshire, England, has been decorated as a souvenir of the building of the Menai Bridge, in Wales, which was completed in 1826.

This earthenware mug is made from clay.

Materials

Many different materials are used to make mugs and plates. As with the making of all products, energy is also used to run the machines that help mine the clay and minerals, and to make and fire the pottery.

Materials used to make mugs and plates

Material	Purpose and qualities
Earthenware clay	Used to make cheap **earthenware pottery** for everyday use.
Stoneware clay	Used to make strong, durable **stoneware pottery**.
Porcelain clay	Used to make white, glassy pottery such as porcelain and bone china.
Minerals such as silica and feldspar	Give porcelain a glassy, **translucent** look.
Glaze made from salt, ash, **metal oxides**, stone-like minerals or clays	Gives a glassy, waterproof coating for the pottery surface, as well as colouring or decorating it.

Guess What!

The essential ingredient in bone china is animal bone. The bone is first cleaned, then heated to very high temperatures and ground finely. It is then added to other minerals to give bone china its white, translucent look.

Canadian ceramic artist Bill Reddick uses a potter's wheel to shape white porcelain clay into a plate.

Mug and plate design

There are many different buyers for mugs and plates. Home owners want casual or formal dinnerware to help decorate their home. Café and hotel owners want sturdy dinnerware that reflects their business.

Designers need to know what their customers want. Traditional designs and patterns for mugs and plates sell well, but customers also look for new designs. Designers need to know about fashion trends.

Big pottery companies have art directors who work with salespeople to design new patterns. First, a clay model of a test mug or plate is produced. Then, a shaped mould creates a copy of it. New ranges are presented at several big trade fairs each year.

Designers also work on the packaging, advertising and display of dinnerware.

Special dinnerware designs are on display at the Meissen porcelain factory, in Germany.

Potters, of England, by
taverns bidden,

Wrought this mug, with
plumbing hidden.

If you be clever and
guess their wit,

With ease then can you
drink from it.

Guess What!

Puzzle mugs were first made by the Greeks in about 200 BCE. They became popular in the 1600s and 1700s. Puzzle mugs had dribble holes and tunnels hidden inside the handle and cup walls, and several drinking spouts. You could drink from just one spout, and only if you covered all the other spouts with your fingers. Otherwise the drink would pour out of the dribble holes and drench you. Puzzle mugs are tricky to make.

This stoneware puzzle mug is sold with instructions from the potter in a sealed envelope on how to drink from it.

Novelty mugs

Mugs are often decorated with novelty designs. Novelty mugs include:

* funny mugs
* mugs with film or cartoon figures on them
* mugs with people's names printed on them
* mugs printed with advertising for companies or services.

From clay to mugs and plates

The process of making everyday objects such as mugs and plates involves a large number of steps. The first stage is mining clay to mould into shapes, and minerals to make powdery glazes to coat them. In the second stage, potters mould the clay into shapes by hand, on a wheel or using machines. The unfired shapes, called **greenware**, are then dried. Next, the mugs and plates are fired in a kiln. They may be decorated and glazed to make them waterproof before being fired again at a higher temperature.

Stage 1: Mining and preparing the clay and glazes

Clay is mined.

Then the clay is mixed with water and minerals.

Next, the clay is pressed into a cylinder, ready for working.

Powdered glazes are made from a range of minerals and chemicals.

Shaping the pottery

The clay is moulded into shape by hand or on a wheel.

For machine-made pottery, the clay is pressed into moulds.

Another way to make pottery is to pour or **slip cast** liquid clay into moulds.

↓

The damp clay greenware may now be decorated.

↓

The greenware is then dried.

Stage 3: Glazing and firing

The dried pottery is **bisque** fired in a kiln.

↓

It may then be glazed, or left unglazed.

↓

Glazed pottery is fired again at a higher temperature to melt the glaze and fuse it to the pottery.

↓

Finally, the unglazed foot of the pottery is polished.

Raw materials for mugs and plates

Clay and glazes for pottery mugs and plates come largely from minerals found in different places.

Most clay for pottery used to come from near where it was made. Now, however, a third of the world's white **kaolin clay** comes from the United States. Other clays are made from mixtures of different minerals, most of which are common around the world.

Glazes are made from mixtures of minerals and chemicals from around the world. Pigments may also be printed or painted on mugs and plates.

Guess What!

In England, kaolin is mined in Devon and Cornwall by aiming high pressure hoses at the wall of the clay pit. The fine clay washes down in a slurry or watery mass.

United Kingdom

Belgium

France

Portugal

EUROPE

Germany
Czech Republic

Italy

AFRICA

ATLANTIC OCEAN

INDIAN OCE

You can see the white kaolin in the walls of this clay pit.

Centres for pottery production

The name 'china' shows that much early pottery came from the country China. From the mid-1700s, England became the main source of pottery mugs and plates, especially from Stoke-on-Trent and nearby pottery towns. Nowadays, some luxury tableware still comes from Europe. China, however, now makes half the world's porcelain. Asia is increasingly producing pottery, since the costs of employing workers there are lower.

Key

- ✪ Important clay-mining countries
- ◆ Important kaolin-mining countries
- ☕ Important porcelain-manufacturing countries
- ☕ Other china-manufacturing countries

ARCTIC OCEAN

China

✪ Japan

Thailand

Singapore

PACIFIC OCEAN

NORTH AMERICA

✪◆ United States of America

ATLANTIC OCEAN

AUSTRALIA

PACIFIC OCEAN

◆ Brazil
SOUTH AMERICA

ATLANTIC OCEAN

OCEAN

This map shows countries that are important to the production of mugs and plates.

ANTARCTICA

Stage 1: Mining and preparing the clay and glazes

Clay is earthy material made of very fine particles. It is very common worldwide. Clay is dug from areas called 'pipes' to be used nearby or sent to other areas if it is special, like the fine white kaolin used in making bone china.

The clay arrives at the factory in powdered form because this is lighter to transport. There it is mixed with water and other minerals, such as sand, quartz and feldspar, to produce different clays.

Depending on their ingredients, different clays produce pottery with different qualities.

✱ Earthenware clays are often reddish.

✱ Stoneware clay is mainly grey or bluish.

✱ Porcelain clays are white, due to kaolin clay, which also makes them hard. They are glassy and translucent due to the mineral feldspar.

In this traditional pug mill, clay is being hammered into a powder.

Children used to work in pottery factories. Robert Hood lived in the English pottery town of Burslem. In 1840, aged 10, he said 'I... have been employed three years... I cannot read; I cannot write; never went to day school... My father is a saucer-maker... Have no mother. My sister stops at home to look after house... I go home to dinner... I am always very tired... and be glad enough to go to bed... Father flogs me sometimes, if I let go a mould or break a saucer; nobody else. Master is very good to me.'

A machine mixes porcelain paste at the Sèvres porcelain factory in France.

Preparing the clay for working

Once the clay is mixed, it is pressed into a hard cake. The clay is then put in a pug mill, which chops and mixes the clay with water until it is elastic and evenly mixed. This prevents air bubbles, which can expand during firing and cause the pottery to break. The clay is then made into a cylinder ready for working.

Making glazes

Glazes are made from a range of minerals, metals and other chemicals. These are ground to a fine powder. The glaze forms a glassy material that sticks to the pottery when it is heated to a high temperature. There is a wide range of glazes, which can look quite different when fired, depending on the temperature, the speed of the firing and how much oxygen is in the air when this happens.

Stage 2: Shaping the pottery

Pottery can be made by hand or by machine.

Handmade pottery

Potters use their hands and other tools to roll, shape, cut and finish mugs and plates. Mugs and plates can be handmade from solid balls, flat slabs or coils of clay.

Potters use a potter's wheel to make matched sets of plates or mugs. They put a clay ball in the turntable centre, and press, squeeze and pull the clay into shape while it spins.

Handles are joined to mugs by a runny clay mixture called slurry or slip.

A craftsman works on a plate at the Sèvres porcelain factory.

Question & Answer

What are jiggering and jolleying?

Jiggering and jolleying are some older methods of shaping pottery with moulds. Flat plates are shaped by jiggering. A shaped tool makes one side of the plate and a plaster mould the other. Hollow containers, such as mugs, are jolleyed. The clay is put into a mould and pressed into shape with a lever.

A worker stacks up pieces of clay ready to be moulded into shape in a roller edge press.

Machine-made pottery

In factories now, there are three main methods of shaping mugs and plates.

* Roller edge pressing involves machines pressing clay into a mould using a tool that is the shape and size of the back of the mug.

* Ram pressing involves moulding a slab of clay between two plates. Another way to do this is to press finely ground clay into moulds and pump water through it at high pressure.

* Pressure slip casting is used for complicated pottery. Liquid clay is poured or injected into plaster moulds. These absorb the water from the shaped objects.

Decorating greenware

Before firing, the damp pottery, called greenware, is trimmed and dried. It can also be decorated in different ways.

The greenware can be rubbed to a polished finish or coated with runny clay slip which is then scratched to reveal some clay underneath. It can also be decorated with printed or painted patterns. More often, greenware is glazed and fired again.

Stage 3: Glazing and firing

Firing pottery makes it hard and strong. Pottery is usually glazed so that it will hold liquids. Glazing also protects and decorates ceramics.

Firing

Firing in a kiln alters clay, turning it into hard pottery. The kiln may be heated by burning wood, coal, oil or gas, or by using electricity.

Early kilns shaped like huge bottles were stacked carefully with pottery, heated and then carefully cooled. Between 20 and 30 per cent of pottery made this way sagged, cracked or failed because of uneven temperatures in the kiln. Now mugs and plates are fired by travelling through tunnel kilns.

Many glazes require pottery to be fired twice. The first firing, between 800 and 1000 degrees Celsius, dries it and fires it to a bisque or biscuit level. After glazing, the pottery is fired again at a higher temperature between 1250 and 1350 degrees Celsius.

Finally, when the pottery has cooled, its unglazed foot is polished by machine.

The pottery is loaded onto trays to be conveyed through the tunnel kiln and fired.

A craftsperson applies glaze onto a bisque pot with a brush.

Some colours produced by different metals in glazes

Metal oxide	Glaze colour
antimony	yellow
copper	green, turquoise, red
cobalt	blue
chrome	greens
gold	ruby red
iron	brown, yellow

Glazing

Glazes are made of salt or minerals mixed to give different colours. Glazes can be applied in either liquid or powdered form. The glaze may be dusted, sprayed or brushed onto the pottery, or the pottery may be dipped into the glaze.

Glaze colours

Colour in glazes is produced by metal oxides. Other glaze minerals, as well as the amount of oxygen in the air, will also affect the colours formed in the glaze. For example, copper will produce blue or green if there is enough oxygen, and beautiful deep blood reds and pinks if there is little oxygen.

Packaging and distribution

Products are packaged to protect them while they are being transported. Packaging also displays the maker's brand and makes products look attractive when they are sold.

Pottery is often sold in sets, such as six mugs, six dinner plates and six bowls. Each piece is heavy, fragile and easily broken, so it needs careful packaging. Items are separated, often in **rigid** cardboard boxes, and wrapped in paper. The cardboard boxes are usually stamped with the name of the maker, the design and other information.

Packaging for expensive tableware is carefully designed to reflect the pattern, and can itself be very beautiful.

Boxes of plates and mugs are packed into bigger cartons, which may then be shrink-wrapped. Then they are shipped in large metal containers.

Workers at a ceramic factory in China package porcelain that will be sent all over the world to be sold.

Distribution

Mugs and plates reach the customer in a number of ways. Factories sell items, and individual potters sell from their studios or at markets.

Most pottery is sent in large quantities by truck, train, plane or ship from the **manufacturer** to a **wholesaler.** The wholesaler sells smaller quantities to **distributors**, especially overseas.

Distributors sell the tableware to a number of department stores, supermarkets and specialty gift and homeware shops.

Crockery for hotels and restaurants is sold through big trade fairs, or directly to the customer by travelling salespeople.

Attractive displays in shops and department stores help persuade customers to buy mugs and plates.

Marketing and advertising

Marketing and advertising are used to promote and sell products.

Royal Doulton ▷ Giftware & Collectables

- Bunnykins
- Character Jugs
- Commemoratives
- Crystal
- Disney Collection
- Elvis
- Figurines
- Pretty Ladies

- Winnie the Pooh

Page [1] 2   Next ▶

Royal Albert Commemoratives & Figurines, Retired - Last Call
$17.49-$115.49
On Sale!

Royal Doulton Abacus Crystal
$21.50-$109.99
On Sale!

Royal Doulton Animal Figurines
$19.99-$99.99
On Sale!

Royal Doulton Bunnykins Figurines
$39.99-$75.00
On Sale!

Royal Doulton Bunnykins Giftware
$31.99-$79.99
On Sale!

Royal Doulton Bunnykins Nurseryware
$5.99-$49.99
On Sale!

Royal Doulton Character Figures
$75.00-$276.49
On Sale!

Royal Doulton Character Jugs, Retired - Last Call
$87.49-$181.99
On Sale!

Royal Doulton Commemoratives, Retired - Last Call
$94.49-$374.49
On Sale!

Royal Doulton Disney Cinderella Showcase Collection
$24.99-$99.99
On Sale!

Royal Doulton Disney Fairies
$19.99-$49.99
On Sale!

Royal Doulton Disney Princesses Showcase Collection
$59.99
On Sale!

The Internet is a great place for manufacturers to promote their entire range of products.

Marketing

Everyone needs ordinary plates and mugs. Some people also buy tableware for special occasions or as wedding gifts. Hotels, restaurants, airlines, hospitals and armies need tough plates and mugs. Elegant restaurants choose stylish tableware that must also be able to cope with dishwashers. Plates and mugs need to be marketed differently to each group of customers.

Generally, pattern is more important than price to individual customers. They can choose traditional or trendy tableware, plain or patterned styles, tough stoneware or delicate china.

Makers promote the company image and brand through **logos**. They can even tell their history in books and videos. Companies work to develop a personal relationship with customers who may then collect a whole range of their products.

Mugs are often given away for advertising. One American TV show awarded mugs to viewers sending in 'morning mugs', photos showing faces of people waking up. Other novelty mugs include **insulated** mugs and travel mugs with lids to prevent spilling.

Advertising

Tableware may be advertised by the maker, who continues manufacturing some patterns and brings out new ones several times a year. It can be advertised in newspapers, magazines and on the Internet.

Tableware is often promoted by stores as part of a whole lifestyle, along with other items such as glassware and linen. Some retailers try to encourage people who are getting married to 'register' a gift list. This tells wedding guests what tableware the bride and groom would prefer to be given as a wedding gift.

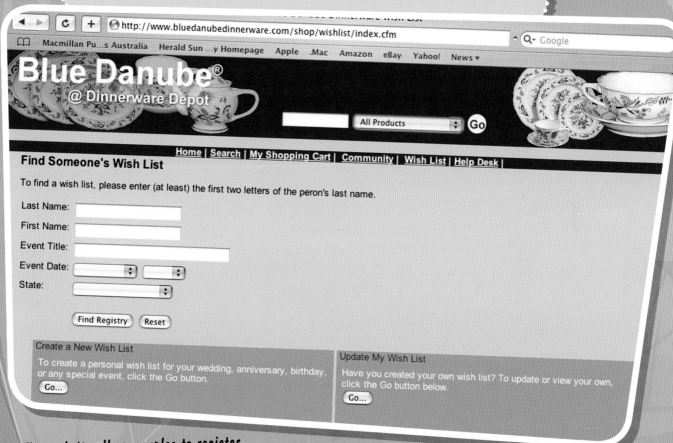

This website allows couples to register a list of tableware they would like to receive as a wedding gift.

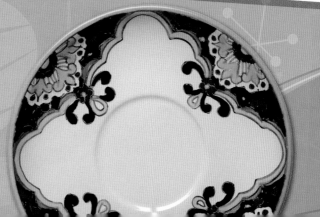

Production of mugs and plates

Products may be made in factories in huge quantities. This is called mass production. They can also be made in small quantities by hand, by skilled craftspeople.

Mass production

Most mugs and plates are mass produced. Mass production enables mugs and plates to look identical. This way, matching sets of crockery can be made.

Mass production is cheaper than making the mugs and plates by hand because fewer people are needed to run the machines that make pottery. Factories, however, are expensive to set up. They need equipment such as pug mills, kilns and computers. Factories also need to use energy, staff and resources efficiently and prevent pollution.

Guess What!

In the late 1700s in England, Josiah Wedgwood was the first potter to sell his work worldwide. It was mass produced, attractive, strong and fashionable. He sold a dinner service of over 950 pieces for Empress Catherine of Russia for less than it cost to make. It gave him huge publicity, however, and brought many more orders.

This drying pottery has been mass produced by pressure slip casting.

Each hand-painted plate from this small pottery in Israel is unique.

Question & Answer

What is a Toby mug?

A Toby jug is a jug in the shape of a stout old man. Toby mugs are a tiny versions of Toby jugs. They are shaped like a figure or face and often look old-fashioned.

Small-scale production

Mugs and plates handmade by potters have individual designs. Even if they match, each one is a little different. They often have rich variations in glaze or designs that make them unique.

Many people enjoy talking to someone who has made their mug, or feeling that they eat from a real work of art every day. Collectors may cherish old pottery, plates by one particular maker, pewter plates with the **patina** of age, or Chinese porcelain that will increase in value.

Some individual unusual mugs include those with heat-sensitive patterns, and even 'pick your nose cups' with different noses printed on their sides. It is possible to choose and order your own words or pattern on a mug through online shops.

Mugs and plates and the environment

Making any product affects the environment. It also affects the people who make the product. It is important to think about the impact of a product through its entire life cycle. This includes getting the raw materials, making the product and disposing of it. Any problems need to be worked on so products can be made in the best ways available.

Mining clay

Like all mining, clay mining can be dangerous. It may also cause environmental problems such as visual and air pollution, earth movement and disruption to nearby plants and animals. Most governments have passed laws on how mining should be done, and companies try to protect their workers from danger.

Manufacturing pottery

Like all factories, those producing mugs and plates can cause problems including air and noise pollution. Most governments have passed laws to protect workers, and responsible employers make factories safe.

Clay mining can scar the landscape.

28

Secondhand mugs and plates from charity shops are a bargain, and it is fun to work out when pieces were made and who might have owned them.

Recycling

Crockery mugs and plates are easy to recycle. Unwanted pottery can be sold or given to charity shops. Sometimes businesses updating their tableware donate their old crockery to schools.

Old pottery can be crushed to help make more pottery, or used in the construction industry as filling material.

Guess What!

There is no need to throw away chipped and cracked mugs and plates. Recycle them as pen and plant containers and fish homes in fish tanks. Make ceramic fragments into jewellery.

Questions to think about

We need to conserve the raw materials used to produce even ordinary objects such as mugs and plates. Making items from **renewable resources**, conserving energy and preventing pollution as much as possible means there will be enough resources in the future and a cleaner environment.

These are some questions you might like to think about:

* What are the advantages of pottery mugs and plates over disposable ones? What are the disadvantages?

* Find an earthenware, stoneware and porcelain mug. How are they different?

* How important to you are the plates and mugs you use every day?

* Look at the maker's mark on a mug or plate. What does it tell you?

* Describe your favourite mug or plate. Why is it special?

* Where does your family's tableware come from?

* Collect some broken pottery, if possible, old pottery. What can you tell from it?

Pottery mugs feel comfortable and friendly, like the earth they are made from.

Glossary

bisque
the French word for biscuit, which is used to describe unglazed pottery after its first firing

ceramics
objects made of clay that has been heated to a high temperature

distributors
shops or wholesalers that have the right to sell a particular product in a certain area

earthenware pottery
pottery fired at low temperatures that water can seep through unless it is glazed

fired
heated in a kiln

glaze
hard glassy finish

greenware
pottery shapes that have not yet been fired

imported
brought into a country from overseas to be sold

insulated
made in such a way as to prevent heat being transferred

kaolin clay
fine white clay

kiln
a very hot oven

logos
images that represent company brands

manufacturer
maker, usually in a factory

metal oxides
substances made up of metals combined with oxygen

moulds
hollow shapes into which liquids are poured to make objects

patina
surface effect produced by age

porcelain
a hard, white ceramic

renewable resources
resources that can easily be grown or made again

rigid
unable to be bent

slip cast
make pottery by pouring liquid clay into a mould that absorbs water

stoneware pottery
hard, stone-like pottery

translucent
letting some light through

waterproof
able to keep water out or in

wholesaler
a business that buys very large quantities of goods and sells them to shops, rather than directly to the consumer

Index